THE STOICISM BOOK OF QUOTES

———

Over 200 Inspirational
Quotations from the Greatest
Stoic Philosophers

NICK BENAS, USMC &
KORTNEY YASENKA, LCMHC

Hatherleigh Press is committed to preserving
and protecting the natural resources of the earth.
Environmentally responsible and sustainable practices are
embraced within the company's mission statement.

Visit us at www.hatherleighpress.com.

THE STOICISM BOOK OF QUOTES

Library of Congress Cataloging-in-Publication Data is available.
ISBN: 978-1-57826-976-1

COVER DESIGN BY CAROLYN KASPER

Printed in the United States
10 9 8 7 6 5 4 3 2

For Chris Canestrari
—Nick

For Helena and Isla, my forever
inspiration and hope for the future
—Kortney

Contents

Introduction

EVERYONE CAN BENEFIT FROM the true meaning and philosophical teachings of stoicism. Having the ability to choose how you react and respond can alleviate anxious and depressive symptoms. The stoic way of thinking allows you to thoughtfully process and accept situations while giving you the power to choose how you react, handle, and cope.

Stoicism allows you to control what you can and let go of what you cannot. It helps you to choose your attitude, to live in the moment, and make sense of your circumstances. Living a more stoic life will give you the opportunity to live a mentally healthier, more balanced, and overall happier life.

The carefully curated quotations compiled here are wonderful tenets to live by and help illustrate specific lessons to improve yourself. We, the authors, have embarked on this exploration of stoic philosophy in our writings, and in our daily professions where we assist individuals on their journeys of personal growth, and recovery. We understand that this odyssey of continued self-education and improvement begins with you. All of us understand that stoicism is one of the many tools you can use to help quell the suffering, to have a better understanding of yourself, and improve your approach to living.

I

A STOIC LIFE

SIMPLY DEFINED, *STOICISM* IS the endurance of pain or hardship without display of feelings and without complaint. Stoicism is a human response to challenge made possible by the fact that we are not merely the byproducts of our circumstances. We are all thinking, self-actualizing beings who have the ability to selectively influence our emotional responses, which in turn shapes how we view the world, ourselves, and others.

Stoicism is known as an *eudaimonistic* theory from the Greek *eudaimonia*, roughly meaning "happiness" or "flourishing." This is meant to be the culmination of human endeavor, or 'end' (*telos*), which the Stoics defined as "living in agreement with nature." Nature is itself a complex and multivalent concept for the Stoics, which in turn means their definition of the goal or final end of human striving is very rich.

For example, their idea of "living in agreement with nature" can also be explained as taking a deeper look into those situations that you *can* control, and those which you cannot. Realizing the need to let go of what you can't control and accepting the facts rather than fighting results in a more harmonious, balanced, and thoughtful life. In modern times, living in agreement with nature means making a conscious effort to make the best of a given situation while being at peace with what you cannot change.

"What then is that which is able to conduct a man? One thing and only one, philosophy."

—MARCUS AURELIUS

"Brave men rejoice in adversity, just as brave soldiers triumph in war."

—SENECA

"A room without books is like a body without a soul."

—CICERO

"If I followed the multitude, I should not have studied philosophy."

—CHRYSIPPUS

"Six mistakes mankind keeps making century after century:

Believing that personal gain is made by crushing others;

Worrying about things that cannot be changed or corrected;

Insisting that a thing is impossible because we cannot accomplish it;

Refusing to set aside trivial preferences;

Neglecting development and refinement of the mind;

Attempting to compel others to believe and live as we do."

—CICERO

"What we achieve inwardly will change outer reality."

—PLUTARCH

"Philosophy is an act of living."

—PLUTARCH

"Nothing is more active than thought, for it travels over the universe, and nothing is stronger than necessity for all must submit to it."

—THALES

"If you have a garden and a library, you have everything you need."

—CICERO

"Time is the wisest of all things that are; for it brings everything to light."

—THALES

"Appearances are a glimpse of the unseen."

—ANAXAGORAS

"He who hesitates is lost."

—CATO

"The Fates guide the person who accepts them and hinder the person who resists them."

—CLEANTHES

"Men would live exceedingly quiet if these two words, mine and thine, were taken away."

—ANAXAGORAS

"A single day among the learned lasts longer than the longest life of the ignorant."

—POSIDONIUS

"As a matter of self-perseveration, a man needs good friends or ardent enemies, for the former instruct him and the latter take him to task."

—DIOGENES

"Each man's soul is his genius."

—XENOCRATES

"Freedom is not procured by a full enjoyment of what is desired, but by controlling the desire."

—EPICTETUS

"To be ignorant of what occurred before you were born is to remain always a child."

—CICERO

"Those whom true love has held, it will go on holding."

—SENECA

II

BEHAVIOR

WHEN YOU HEAR THE phrase "kind behavior and expressions of gratitude" you will, most likely, think of being kind to others and expressing your gratitude for others. While this is extremely useful and beneficial, it is equally important to be kind to yourself and show gratitude to yourself. Numerous studies have shown the positive impact kindness and gratitude have on your mental well-being and quality of life. Activities like keeping a gratitude journal and practicing random acts of kindness help you remember the good in life and help you reflect on positive situations and experiences.

Strive to combat criticism with kindness and take control of your life's situation. Kindness and gratitude are always options and you have the choice to demonstrate both. True strength is to be found in kindness, so begin and end each day by identifying one thing for which you are grateful. It's a simple act that produces significant benefits.

"Gratitude is not only the greatest of virtues,
but the parent of all others."

—CICERO

"Be kind, for everyone you meet is fighting a
harder battle."

—PLATO

"All cruelty springs from weakness."

—SENECA

"If someone succeeds in provoking you, realize that your mind is complicit in the provocation."

—EPICTETUS

"Be tolerant with others and strict with yourself."

—MARCUS AURELIUS

"Love is born into every human being; it calls back the halves of our original nature together; it tries to make one out of two and heal the wound of human nature."

—PLATO, *THE SYMPOSIUM*

"No man is more unhappy than he who never faces adversity. For he is not permitted to prove himself."

—SENECA

"Speak the truth as you see it. But with kindness. With humility."

—MARCUS AURELIUS

"Have I done something for the common good? Then I share in the benefits."

—MARCUS AURELIUS

"In marriage, there must be complete companionship and concern for each other on the part of both husband and wife, in health and in sickness and at all times, because they entered upon the marriage for this reason as well as to produce offspring. When such caring for one another is perfect, and the married couple provides it for one another, and each strives to outdo the other, then this is marriage as it ought to be and deserving of emulation, since it is a noble union. But when one partner looks to his own interests alone and neglects the other's, or (by Zeus) the other is so minded that he lives in the same house, but keeps his mind on what is outside it, and does not wish to pull together with his partner or to cooperate, then inevitably the union is destroyed, and although they live together their common interests fare badly, and either they finally get divorced from one another or they continue on in an existence that is worse than loneliness."

—RUFUS

"What progress, you ask, have I made? I have begun to be a friend to myself."

—HECATO OF RHODES

"In your actions, don't procrastinate. In your conversations, don't confuse. In your thoughts, don't wander. In your soul, don't be passive or aggressive. In your life, don't be all about business."

—MARCUS AURELIUS

"I begin to speak only when I'm certain what I'll say isn't better left unsaid."

—CATO

"We have two ears and one mouth, so we should listen more than we say."

—ZENO, QUOTED BY
DIOGENES LAËRTIUS

"Man's character is his fate."

—HERACLITUS, *FRAGMENTS*

"You will earn the respect of all if you begin by earning the respect of yourself. Don't expect to encourage good deeds in people conscious of your own misdeeds."

—MUSONIUS RUFUS

"People often say what is right and do what is wrong; but nobody can be in the wrong if he is doing what is right."

—XENOPHON, *CONVERSATIONS OF SOCRATES*

"Never discourage anyone…who continually makes progress, no matter how slow."

—PLATO

"Most people, when they are set upon looking into other people's affairs, never turn to examine themselves."

—XENOPHON, *CONVERSATIONS OF SOCRATES*

"Quality is not an act, it is a habit."

—ARISTOTLE

"I will reveal to you a love potion, without medicine, without herbs, without any witch's magic; if you want to be loved, then love."

—HECATO OF RHODES

"Virtue is the health of the soul."

—ARISTO OF CHIO

"Kindness is unconquerable, so long as it is without flattery or hypocrisy. For what can the most insolent man do to you, if you contrive to be kind to him, and if you have the chance gently advise and calmly show him what is right...and point this out tactfully and from a universal perspective."

—MARCUS AURELIUS

III

MINDSET

"MIND OVER MATTER" IS a powerful expression. Your ability to consciously control your mindset is what makes you mentally tough and ready for life's challenges. The secret to achieving this resilient state lies in taking control of your thoughts and allowing your thoughts to control your behaviors, not the other way around. Your ability to take control of your emotional responses and live a stoic-inspired life is the secret to success, to your happiness, and to your improved well-being.

When you are able to see situations as opportunities and emotional responses as conscious choices—when you realize things don't happen *to* you but rather *with* you—your outlook completely changes. How you see your situation affects and influences how you feel about that situation. You are not merely a byproduct of your circumstances. You are a choosing being who has the ability to determine your emotional responses, which in turn shapes how you view the world, yourselves, and others.

But learning to change your perspectives takes practice—practice which will in turn help increase your self-confidence. By practicing cognitive restructuring, you can retrain your brain and create new habits that will make you the master of any situation. When choosing how you feel and react becomes your choice, you will feel more in control.

"Don't hope that events will turn out the way you want, welcome events in whichever way they happen: this is the path to peace."

—EPICTETUS

"Nothing beautiful without struggle."

—PLATO, *THE REPUBLIC*

"Recognize that if something is humanly possible, you can do it too."

—MARCUS AURELIUS

"The worst type of man behaves as badly in his waking life as some men do in their dreams."

—PLATO, *THE REPUBLIC*

"Ask yourself at every moment, is this necessary?"

—MARCUS AURELIUS

"You have to assemble your life yourself, action by action."

—MARCUS AURELIUS

"Rule your mind or it will rule you."

—HORACE

"Love is a serious mental disease."

—PLATO, *PHAEDRUS*

"The greater the difficulty, the more glory in surmounting it. Skillful pilots gain their reputations from storms and tempests."

—EPICTETUS

"Don't be overheard complaining...not even to yourself."

—MARCUS AURELIUS

"Everything hangs on one's thinking...a man is as unhappy as he has convinced himself he is."

—SENECA

"We are more often frightened than hurt; and we suffer more in imagination than in reality."

—SENECA

"External things are not the problem. It's your assessment of them, which you can erase right now."

—MARCUS AURELIUS

"It is not the man who has too little, but the man who craves more, that is poor."

—SENECA

"Today, I escaped from anxiety. Or, no; I discarded it, because it was within me, in my own perceptions—not outside."

—MARCUS AURELIUS

"The whole future lies in uncertainty: live immediately."

—SENECA

"Man is not worried by real problems so much as by his imagined anxieties about real problems."

—EPICTETUS

"No man can have a peaceful life who thinks too much about lengthening it."

—SENECA

"People are frugal in guarding their personal property; but as soon as it comes to squandering time they are most wasteful of the one thing in which it is right to be stingy."

—SENECA

"First say to yourself what you would be; and then do what you have to do."

—EPICTETUS

"Don't explain your philosophy. Embody it."

—EPICTETUS

"Nothing, to my way of thinking, is a better proof of a well ordered mind than a man's ability to stop just where he is and pass some time in his own company."

—SENECA

"There is only one way to happiness and that is to cease worrying about things which are beyond the power or our will."

—EPICTETUS

"Every hour, focus your mind attentively...
on the performance of the task in hand, with
dignity, human sympathy, benevolence and
freedom, and leave aside all other thoughts.
You will achieve this, if you perform each
action as if it were your last."

—MARCUS AURELIUS

IV

TOXICITY

TOXICITY REFERS TO THE quality of being very harmful or unpleasant to oneself. Toxic emotions and the manifestations of certain behaviors can be found in almost every aspect of your life, but only if you allow it. The teachings of the great Stoics emphasize the notion of accepting what you cannot control.

By living the stoic life, you are in total control of your own mental hygiene. You have the choice to limit the amount of destructive behaviors within you and the amount you inflict onto others. This makes you responsible for your own toxicity. The harmfulness can significantly impact your daily functioning, and the regulation of your moods and emotions. You must identify the origin, acknowledge and then accept that you have the power to change.

Remind yourself that allowing toxicity to live within you relinquishes control over your own life and well-being. Choose to live a toxic free lifestyle and let the great Stoics be your guide.

"Excess in anything becomes a fault."

—SENECA

"It is essential that we not respond impulsively...
take a moment before reacting, and you will
find it easier to maintain control."

—EPICTETUS

"Deaths that are greater, greater portions gain."

—HERACLITUS

"The awake share a common world, but the asleep turn aside into private worlds."

—HERACLITUS

"If it's endurable, then endure it, stop complaining."

—MARCUS AURELIUS

"If it is not right, do not do it, if it is not true, do not say it."

—MARCUS AURELIUS

"How does it help…to make troubles heavier by bemoaning them?"

—SENECA

"Waste no more time arguing what a good man should be. Be one."

—MARCUS AURELIUS

"Don't allow yourself to be heard any longer griping about public life, not even with your own ears!"

—MARCUS AURELIUS

"We must take a higher view of all things, and bear with them more easily: it better becomes a man to scoff at life than to lament over it."

—SENECA

"Death is not the worst that can happen to men."

—PLATO

"People are like dirt. They can either nourish you and help you grow as a person or they can stunt your growth and make you wilt and die."

—PLATO

"The first rule is to keep an untroubled spirit. The second is to look things in the face and know them for what they are."

—MARCUS AURELIUS

"Men seek out retreats for themselves in the country, by the seaside, on the mountains… nowhere can a man find a retreat more peaceful or more free from trouble than his own soul."

—MARCUS AURELIUS

"Order your soul. Reduce your wants."

—AUGUSTINE OF HIPPO

"Men are of little worth. Their brief lives last a single day. They cannot hold elusive pleasure fast; Ii melts away. All laurels wither; all illusions fade; Hopes have been phantoms, shade on air-built shade since time began."

—SOPHOCLES

"To bear trials with a calm mind robs misfortune of its strength and burden."

—SENECA

"Misfortune nobly born is good fortune."

—MARCUS AURELIUS

"If you are distressed by anything external, the pain is not due to the thing itself, but to your estimate of it; and this, you have the power to revoke at any moment."

—MARCUS AURELIUS

"The willing are led by fate, the reluctant dragged."

—CLEANTHES

"All that exists is the seed of what will emerge from it."

—MARCUS AURELIUS

V

MORTALITY

WHILE MORTALITY MAY AT first seem like a negative topic, it should instead be seen as a chance to embrace life, be grateful for what you have, and come to terms with the fact that nothing is forever. The idea of mortality as an ending point should be looked at in a positive manner. Time is finite; for this reason, it should be viewed as a precious resource. Learning to rethink mortality is a perfect example about the Stoic practice of changing your mindset, expressing gratitude, and accepting and living in agreement with your circumstances.

Acceptance of your mortality will allow you to live each day to the fullest and appreciate each moment. Since mortality is something you cannot control (in most circumstances), you must learn to view it with a new perspective and allow that new perspective to enrich your life, not hinder it. Acceptance and acknowledgment of what is to come and fully appreciating being in the present will allow you to live a more mindful and purposeful life. Always accept reality and focus on making the most out of any situation.

"Well-being is attained little by little, and nevertheless is no little thing itself."

—ZENO OF CITIUM

"All the gold which is under or upon the earth is not enough to give in exchange for virtue."

—PLATO

"Ask yourself at every moment, is this necessary?"

—MARCUS AURELIUS

"Never let the future disturb you. You will meet it, if you have to, with the same weapons of reason which today arm you against the present."

—MARCUS AURELIUS

"Rashness belongs to youth; prudence to old age."

—MARCUS TULLIUS CICERO

"Cowards die many times before their death."

—JULIUS CAESAR

"Think of yourself as dead. You have lived your life. Now take what's left and live it properly."

—MARCUS AURELIUS

"For a man to conquer himself is the first and noblest of all victories."

—PLATO

"Do not spoil what you have by desiring what you have not."

—EPICURUS

"The only thing I know is that I know nothing."

—SOCRATES

"There is no easy way from the earth to the stars."

—SENECA

"The greater the difficulty, the more glory in surmounting it."

—EPICURUS

"The greatest obstacle to living is expectancy, which hangs upon tomorrow, and loses today."

—SENECA

"To move the world, we must first move ourselves."

—SOCRATES

"Only the dead have seen the end of war."

—PLATO

"Mortal as I am, I know that I am born for a day. But when I follow at my pleasure the serried multitude of the stars in their circular course, my feet no longer touch the earth."

—PTOLEMY

"Since every man dies, it is better to die with distinction than to live long."

—MUSONIUS RUFUS

"Let us prepare our minds as if we'd come to the very end of life. Let us postpone nothing."

—SENECA

"Imagine that the keeper of a huge, strong beast notices what makes it angry, what it desires, how it has to be approached and handled, the circumstances and the conditions under which it becomes particularly fierce or calm, what provokes its typical cries, and what tones of voice make it gentle or wild. Once he's spent enough time in the creature's company to acquire all this information, he calls it knowledge, forms it into a systematic branch of expertise, and starts to teach it, despite total ignorance, in fact, about which of the creature's attitudes and desires is commendable or deplorable, good, or bad, moral or immoral. His usage of all these terms simply conforms to the great beast's attitudes, and he describes things as good or bad according to its likes and dislikes, and can't justify his usage of the terms any further, but describes as right and good the things which are merely indispensable, since he hasn't realized and can't explain to anyone else how vast a gulf there is between necessity and goodness."

—PLATO, *THE REPUBLIC*

"He who fears death will never do anything worth of a man who is alive."

—SENECA

"Courage is knowing what not to fear."

—PLATO

"Death smiles at us all, but all a man can do is smile back."

—MARCUS AURELIUS

"Well begun is half done."

—ARISTOTLE

"Your days are numbered. Use them to throw open the windows of your soul to the sun. If you do not, the sun will soon set, and you with it."

—MARCUS AURELIUS

VI

REASONING

PIERRE HADOT SAID IT best when he stated, "What defined a Stoic above all else was the choice of a life in which every thought, every desire, and every action would be guided by no other law than that of universal Reason." Your well-being is based on living in accordance with this universal reason, as it is what creates a life of balance and virtue. This understanding of reason is what guides the Stoic in everyday decisions and actions.

Reason is what allows you to understand perspectives and situations. It's what determines, through thoughtful processing, how you want to respond. Reason is what gives you the ability to actively chose your response to situations and allows you to gain a sense of control over your cognition and emotions. When you live by reason, you will live a life of less resistance, a happier life and one where you feel more in control by acknowledging what you cannot control. It is through reasoning that you become a master of your life and reach your ultimate well-being. Reason is what helps you achieve a higher understanding of nature, yourself, and to live a more ethical life.

"We can easily forgive a child who is afraid of the dark; the real tragedy of life is when men are afraid of the light."

—PLATO

"There could be no justice, unless there were also injustice; no courage, unless there were cowardice; no truth, unless there were falsehood."

—CHRYSIPPUS

"If you want rainbow, you have to deal with the rain."

—AUGUSTUS

"The tranquility that comes when you stop caring what they say. Or think or do. Only what you do."

—MARCUS AURELIUS

"Not what we have but what we enjoy constitutes our abundance."

—EPICURUS

"Nothing exists except atoms and free space, everything else is opinion."

—DEMOCRITUS

"Before a crowd, the ignorant are more persuasive than the educated."

—ARISTOTLE

"The truth is like a lion; you don't have to defend it. Let it loose; it will defend itself."

—AUGUSTINE OF HIPPO

"If God listened to the prayers of men, all men would quickly have perished: for they are forever praying for evil against one another."

—EPICURUS

"Wisdom outweighs any wealth."

—SOPHOCLES

"In anger we should refrain both from speech and action."

—PYTHAGORAS

"First learn the meaning of what you say, and then speak."

—EPICTETUS

"I do not know whether I shall make progress; but I should prefer to lack success rather than to lack faith."

—SENECA

"You have power over your mind - not outside events. Realise this, and you will find strength."

—MARCUS AURELIUS

"If a friend feels upset by you, be the first to try to put things right."

—MARCUS AURELIUS

"Healing is a matter of time, but it is sometimes also a matter of opportunity."

—HIPPOCRATES

"Dogs and philosophers do the greatest good and get the fewest rewards."

—DIOGENES

"Above all things, respect yourself."

—PYTHAGORAS

"The mind that is anxious about future events is miserable."

—SENECA

"To study philosophy is nothing but to prepare oneself to die."

—CICERO

"A bad feeling is a commotion of the mind repugnant to reason and against nature."

—ZENO

VII

FAILURE

FAILURE IS AN EXPECTED part of life. It's how you deal with these setbacks that determines how they will affect you. The key to living a Stoic life is to find the successes in the midst of failure, the silver linings in a setback. It's your perspective that makes a situation either positive or negative. Whether or not you can see the good in experiences—while understanding and accepting the situation—is what will ultimately make you a stronger person.

Instead of allowing detrimental situations to define you and your attitude, you must realize that as a human being you have the ability to choose how you respond to situations and that the way in which you perceive these challenges has a tremendous effect on the quality of your life. Anyone who has suffered a great trauma knows firsthand that you cannot control or change what has happened, but you *can* control how you cope with the incident. Often times, individuals who have been through the greatest challenges have markedly more positive outlooks than those whose lives have been comparatively easy.

The goal of a life well-lived is not to eliminate failure, but rather to use our failures as information and gain an understanding as to why we failed, what went wrong. When you can do that, you can alter your viewpoint which will make it easier for you to choose how you respond in the future. Being stoic does not mean you don't feel; it simply means you are accepting your failure and choosing how to react in a way that will benefit you, rather than hinder you. Acceptance is a vital part in making the most out of your situations.

"Better to do a little well than a great deal badly."

—SOCRATES

"He suffers more than necessary, who suffers before it is necessary."

—MARCUS AURELIUS

"No man ever steps in the same river twice, for it's not the same river and he's not the same man."

—HERACLITUS

"How does it help...to make troubles heavier by bemoaning them?"

—SENECA

"What we do now echoes in eternity."

—MARCUS AURELIUS

"The soul is dyed the color of its thoughts. Think only on those things that are in line with your principles and can bear the light of day. The content of your character is your choice. Day by day, what you do is who you become. Your integrity is your destiny—it is the light that guides your way."

—HERACLITUS

"If you accomplish something good with hard work, the labor passes quickly, but the good endures; if you do something shameful in pursuit of pleasure, the pleasure passes quickly, but the shame endures."

—MUSONIUS RUFUS

"Reject your sense of injury and the injury itself disappears."

—MARCUS AURELIUS

"Pleasures, when they go beyond a certain limit, are but punishments."

—MARCUS AURELIUS

"Wealth is able to buy the pleasures of eating, drinking and other sensual pursuits—yet can never afford a cheerful spirit or freedom from sorrow."

—MUSONIUS RUFUS, *MUSONIUS RUFUS ON HOW TO LIVE*

"Sometimes even to live is an act of courage."

—SENECA

"Rather fail with honor than succeed by fraud."

—SOPHOCLES

"It is not death that a man should fear, but he should fear never beginning to live."

—MARCUS AURELIUS

"The problem creates the solution. What stands in the way becomes the way."

—MARCUS AURELIUS

"Bitter are the roots of study, but how sweet their fruit."

—CATO

"The foundation of every state is the education of its youth."

—DIOGENES

"Be indifferent to what makes no difference."

—MARCUS AURELIUS

"It is greed to do all the talking but to not want to listen at all."

—DEMOCRITUS

"As fire tests gold, so misfortunate tests brave men."

—SENECA

"A fool is known by his speech; and a wise man by silence."

—PYTHAGORAS

"Talk sense to a fool and he calls you foolish."

—EURIPIDES

"Look back over the past, with its changing empires that rose and fell, and you can foresee the future, too."

—MARCUS AURELIUS

"Think your way through difficulties: harsh conditions can be softened, restricted ones can be widened, and heavy ones can weigh less on those who know how to bear them."

—SENECA

"Nothing is needed by fools, for they do not understand how to use anything, but are in want of everything."

—MARCUS AURELIUS

"Here is a rule to remember in future, when anything tempts you to feel bitter: not, 'This is misfortune,' but, 'To bear this worthily is good fortune.'"

—MARCUS AURELIUS

VIII

NATURE

THE STOIC'S ULTIMATE GOAL is to live in accordance with nature—to be one with nature and live harmoniously. To appreciate and gain an understanding of your place in the world, to practice your ability to see things greater than yourself and live a virtuous life; living according to nature is living your best life.

Living your best life is done by maximizing your potential—by recognizing the difference between what you can control and what is out of your control. You must be honest with yourself and others and be willing to seek the truth in every circumstance. By doing so, you must also see challenges as a way to progress and not as a setback. Seek to find the good in every situation and use it as a teaching tool. Let nature be your guiding force and your moral compass on your positive pathway in life.

"When a dog is tied to a cart, if it wants to follow, it is pulled and follows, making its spontaneous act coincide with necessity. But if the dog does not follow, it will be compelled in any case. So it is with men, too: even if they don't want to, they will be compelled to follow what is destined."

—ZENO

"Glory follows virtue as if it were its shadow."

—CICERO

"He needs little who desires but little."

—CLEANTHES

"The fates lead the willing but drag the unwilling."

—CLEANTHES

"The first step: Don't be anxious. Nature controls it all."

—MARCUS AURELIUS

"The goal of life is living in agreement with Nature."

—ZENO

"The greatest wealth is to live content with little."

—PLATO

"It is the power of the mind to be unconquerable."

—SENECA

"Except our own thoughts, there is nothing absolutely in our power."

—DESCARTES

"Wise people are in want of nothing, and yet need many things."

—CHRYSIPPUS

"The fool's life is empty of gratitude and full of fears; its course lies wholly toward the future."

—EPICURUS

"Before you heal someone, ask him if he's willing to give up the things that make him sick."

—HIPPOCRATES

"Nothing truly stops you. Nothing truly holds you back. For your own will is always within your control."

—EPICTETUS

"Contentment is natural wealth, luxury is artificial poverty."

—SOCRATES

"Seek not the good in external things; seek it in yourselves."

—EPICTETUS

"Concern should drive us into action and not into depression. No man is free who cannot control himself."

—PYTHAGORAS

"No man is hurt by himself."

—DIOGENES

"Knowing yourself is the beginning of all wisdom."

—ARISTOTLE

"Confine yourself to the present."

—MARCUS AURELIUS

"One man is worth thousand if he is extraordinary."

—HERACLITUS

"Why should we pay so much attention to what the majority thinks?"

—SOCRATES

"Man conquers the world by conquering himself."

—ZENO OF CITIUM

"Nature does nothing uselessly."

—ARISTOTLE

IX

RULES FOR LIVING

THE STOICS' BASIC RULES of living emphasize the importance of viewing yourself and
the world objectively while living in acceptance
with nature. To view the world objectively
allows you to see situations free from personal
emotions and subjectivity.

Another basic rule is to not allow yourself
to be controlled by external circumstances, but
instead to focus on what you can control while
being fully in the present moment. Do not allow
yourself to think too far into the future or rumi-
nate too much about the past.

Stoic living results in a life of resilience, con-
fidence, and calmness. These three qualities can
help in every aspect of life, and in any situation.
Put into practice the Stoic rules for living and

you will be on your way to a more balanced sense of well-being. Remember "the why" and purpose of the things you do and let that direct you to reaching your full potential.

"As long as you live, keep learning how to live."

—SENECA

"Devote the rest of your life to making progress."

—EPICTETUS

"People who labor all their lives but have no purpose to direct every thought and impulse toward are wasting their time-even when hard at work."

—MARCUS AURELIUS

"The essence of philosophy is that a man should so live that his happiness shall depend as little as possible on external things."

—EPICTETUS

"And you can also commit injustice by doing nothing."

—MARCUS AURELIUS

"If a man knows not to which port he sails, no wind is favorable."

—SENECA

"You become what you give your attention to."

—EPICTETUS

"At dawn, when you have trouble getting out of bed, tell yourself: I have to go to work—as a human being. What do I have to complain of, if I'm going to do what I was born for—the things I was brought into the world to do? Or is this what I was created for? To huddle under the blankets and stay warm?"

—MARCUS AURELIUS

"Wait for that wisest of all counselors: time."

—PERICLES

"The best livelihood (particularly for the strong) is earning a living from the soil, whether you own your land or not. Many can support their families by farming land owned by the state or private landowners. Some even get rich through hard work with their own hands. The earth repays those who cultivate her, both justly and well, multiplying what she received—endowing in abundance all the necessities of life to anyone willing to work—and all this without violating your dignity or self-respect!"

—MUSONIUS RUFUS, *MUSONIUS RUFUS ON HOW TO LIVE*

"Just that you do the right thing. The rest doesn't matter."

—MARCUS AURELIUS

"The heaviest penalty for declining to rule is to be ruled by someone inferior to yourself."

—PLATO, *THE REPUBLIC*

"Do not train a child to learn by force or harshness; but direct them to it by what amuses their minds, so that you may be better able to discover with accuracy the peculiar bent of the genius of each."

—PLATO

"The measure of a man is what he does with power."

—PLATO

"Human behavior flows from three main sources: desire, emotion, and knowledge."

—PLATO

"There is truth in wine and children."

—PLATO, *PHAEDRUS*

"If you don't have consistent goal in life, you can't live it in a consistent way."

—MARCUS AURELIUS

"You are well aware that it is not numbers or strength that bring the victories in war. No, it is when one side goes against the enemy with the gods' gift of a stronger morale that their adversaries, as a rule, cannot withstand them. I have noticed this point too, my friends, that in soldiering the people whose one aim is to keep alive usually find a wretched and dishonorable death, while the people who, realizing that death is the common lot of all men, make it their endeavour to die with honour, somehow seem more often to reach old age and to have a happier life when they are alive. These are facts which you too should realize (our situation demands it) and should show that you yourselves are brave men and should call on the rest to do likewise."

—XENOPHON, *THE PERSIAN EXPEDITION*

"Let your speech be better than silence, or be silent."

—DIONYSIUS

"The greatest remedy for anger is delay."

—SENECA

"Having the fewest wants, I am nearest to the gods."

—SOCRATES

"It is thus with farming: if you do one thing late, you will be late in all your work."

—CATO THE ELDER

"Enjoy present pleasures in such a way as not to injure future ones."

—SENECA

X

MASTERY

SELF-MASTERY IS A VITAL component of freedom. If you do not have mastery over yourself, you will never be truly free from conflict, dilemma, or self-doubt. Freedom and self-mastery allow you to be self-determining, which in turn empowers you to be the master of your own life, your own journey, and your own destiny. The skill of mastery gives you the ability to control your emotions, your perspectives, and your reactions, while self-mastery makes it capable for you to determine your own actions and not allow external actions to control you.

Learning how to be a master of your emotions frees you from negative mood dysregulation while increasing your ability to better manage your reactions and coping strategies.

Self-mastery is seen as the final goal in living a Stoic life. To have mastery over yourself is to truly know and accept the things you can and cannot control.

"The first and greatest victory is to conquer yourself."

—HIEROCLES

"Pleasure in the job puts perfection in the work."

—ARISTOTLE

"A gift consists not in what is done or given, but in the intention of the giver or doer."

—SENECA

"He who conquers his passions is master of his own worlds."

—HIEROCLES

"He who has equipped himself for the whole of life does not need to be advised concerning each separate thing, because he is now trained to meet his problem as a whole; for he knows not merely how he should live with his wife or his son, but how he should live aright."

—ARISTO OF CHIOS

"The highest good is not to seek to do good
but to allow yourself to become it."

—HIEROCLES

"Wishing to be friends is quick work, but
friendship is a slow-ripening fruit."

—ARISTOTLE

"As it is with a play, so it is with life - what
matters is not how long the acting lasts, but
how good it is."

—SENECA

"So it is with men too: even if they don't want to, they will be compelled to follow what is destined."

—ZENO

"Mastery of reading and writing requires a master. Still more so life."

—MARCUS AURELIUS

"Anyone who can make you angry becomes your master."

—EPICTETUS

"Accept whatever comes to you woven in the pattern of your destiny, for what could more aptly fit your needs?"

—MARCUS AURELIUS

"Attach yourself to what is spiritually superior, regardless of what other people think or do. Hold to your true aspirations no matter what is going on around you."

—EPICTETUS

"A humble art affords us daily bread."

—NERO

"Hang on to your youthful enthusiasms you'll be able to use them better when you're older."

—SENECA

"To be even-minded is the greatest virtue."

—HERACLITUS

"From this instant on, vow to stop disappointing yourself, separate yourself from the mob. Decide to be extraordinary and do what you need to do—now."

—EPICTETUS

"He who sweats more in training bleeds less in war."

—GREEK PROVERB

"If you want to improve, be content to be thought foolish and stupid."

—EPICTETUS

"He has the most who is content with the least."

—DIOGENES

Final Thoughts

POWERFUL WORDS CAN PRY open new beliefs and reexamine old ones, leaving a lasting impression. These words may in turn allow you to gain new acceptances and foster new reasoning.

When was the last time you memorized a string of words or numbers? Was it for grade school tests or before the onset of mobile phone technology? It's hard to imagine there was a time in history where you had to be committed to learning important phone numbers to dial. Those seven to ten digits of recall was your code to connect. The orators of the past were reliant on their memory to deliver and pass on wisdom from the great stoic philosophers. We encourage you to take the personal challenge and remember your favorite passages. Embody the joy and self-satisfaction when you're able to conjure during a deep conversation at a cocktail party, or to assist a dear friend in the throes of anxiety.

Lastly, let us not forget our own mortality and we must accept the terms that nothing lasts forever. All we have is right now, so please protect your most precious asset.

About the Authors

Nick Benas grew up in Guilford, Connecticut. He is a former United States Marine Sergeant and Iraqi Combat Veteran with a background in Martial Arts (2nd Dan Black Belt in Tae Kwon-Do and Green Belt Instructor in the Marine Corps Martial Arts Program). Nick attended Southern Connecticut State University for his undergraduate degree in Sociology and his M.S. in Public Policy. He has been featured for his business success and entrepreneurship by more than 50 major media outlets, including Entrepreneur Magazine, Men's Health, ABC, FOX, ESPN, and CNBC. His passion lies in writing and serving Veterans.

Kortney Yasenka, LCMHC, is a licensed clinical mental health counselor who provides individual, family, and group therapy, as well as life coaching services. Kortney is certified in trauma focused cognitive behavioral therapy and incorporates physical activity and eco-therapy into counseling and coaching sessions. She has a Masters in Counseling Psychology with a concentration in Health Psychology from Northeastern University. With over 15 years of experience, Kortney has worked in community mental health, school systems, and private practice.

Also by Nick Benas

The Warrior's Book of Virtues
Mental Health Emergencies
Tactical Mobility
Warrior Wisdom
The Resilient Warrior